Telekinesis: A Beginner's Step-By-Step Guide To Developing Telekinesis (Psychokinesis)

Table of Contents

Introduction to Telekinesis

For very many years Telekinesis has been faced with a lot of mockery and skepticism. Quite often individuals never let such tricks and ideas get into their mind due to the fact that they have never seen people doing them. Although this is the fact, a number of people still believe in Telekinesis, even if no science has been done to prove it. This guide has been created in a step by step procedure to guide you as a beginner in Telekinesis. If you have mind and understanding you will find it suiting you very well. This guide has been broken down to three phases with 15 steps guide.

Phase One: Getting The Time Zone

Step - 1:

In this step you will be required to work on your skills of visualization. This is actually one of the major exercises that you have to undertake when it comes to Telekinesis. It can be visualization of yourself or the objects that are around your vicinity. Unless you have back up skills to this exercise, it can work out very well. You have to start visualizing for it to work! To put it in a simple way, visualizing is just like meditating. The results are seen in the mind but not in the real life situation, in turn you will aim at having them plying out in the real life situation.

As a beginner start with visualization of the objects which are small. Here you should focus on each and every detail, that is; taste, color nuances, fell as well as smell. Work on each of the mentioned areas to ensure that at the end of it you can make a visualization of all the scenes while having yourself in them.

Step - 2:

In this step you will be working on meditation. For any person who is well versed with the Telekinesis world, meditation plays a key role in development of superhuman skills to an individual. You have to ensure that your brain is fully clear- that is 100% clear and fresh so that you can direct the energy of your body to the objects that are around your vicinity. This means that you ought to ensure that there are no any other thoughts that distract, disrupt or pervade you in the process of channeling you energy and clear thought. To develop this skill in a quicker way, meditation plays a key role.

In our current lifestyle is practically a great thing to carry out many things at ones. We have very many things to look at and do, such that if you won't drop the very many unnecessary ones you might end up doing wrong in all of them. During the process of meditation you give your mind a chance to make an escape of this modern lifestyle by making all the unnecessary thoughts go away. At the end of it your mental power will take the center stage of only a single thing.

Step - 3:

After making a full meditation of your mind, and ensuring your thoughts are clear, you now have to open your mind. This is the third step. You cannot get any results in Telekinesis just like in hypnosis when you have a mind which is closed. This is a skeptic mind and can ruin you from achieving the desired results. Such that when you have the thought that you can't do anything, you will actually end up not doing anything. Give it more than 100%, by ignoring the sciences behind it as well as naysayers. Surely it can be possible that there is no anything that might happen but in any at every undertaking in life if you don't let things to happen they won't happen at all.

In this case you don't have to doubt anything generally; you don't have to the possibility of things happening in the real life when you are passionately wanting then to happen. Positive results are bred by positive thoughts, and contrary to this, negative results in the same way are bred by negative thoughts. Thoughts breed themselves in your life a single negative thought can spur up thousands of similar thoughts. This turns you into a skeptic. When you have the belief that you can undertake something comfortably it is then the time that you can actually do it.

Step - 4:
This step calls for patience. Nothing in life happen in an eye blink- even in gambling you have to gamble first for you to win the great amount of cash or reward in an eye blink. Long ago Telekinesis was practiced in years for one to fully get done and have the skills

behind it. It was not days, nor months but years. Here you might practice thousand of time prior to stumbling this magical behind mixture of energy effectively. You will have to keep at it as it is never known where or how it can strike.

In this case there is no any other reward but waiting the real kicker to happen. Telekinesis is very divergent from normal life situations like guitar playing or weight loss programs where you can actually see and feel the gradual progress of the process at glance. In this situation you may practice daily for very many days without feeling anything happening, but it will be until one day that something will happen. This is just a matter of having all your senses dedicated to it and finally realizing the results.

Step - 5:

Here you have to relax. This means that both your body and mind should be relaxed. In case you are undergoing a meditation process; there will be no any big deal I this case. Imagine a case where you are trying to dispel all the excess thoughts and channeling your energy while you are still strung on matters about your relationship, job, or the things that were said by a given person in school. This is making things impossible. You have to relax and let everything go. This means that all your thoughts have to be dedicated to this very moment in a fully and truly way. In any case you can't have your brain in various situations.

To get rid of the daily life stresses, yoga plays a key role. Thus, as an additional practice to meditation you ought to take a few minutes of your daily time to dedicate to yourself- this is general exercise. You can have around half an hour of your time in this- it will make the rest of your day very easier.

Step - 6:

Here you have to "convince yourself" that the manipulator- who is you and the system- that is the object, have got the same energy. In this case you should abandon the scientific fact that the two are different. This is all the basis and core behind Telekinesis; that is the object and you are the same and one. Abandon any other belief. Believe the fact that all the matter on earth and universe in general were one at a given moment as stardust. With this fact you will actually move the object that is before you due to the fact that it has an extension that is natural from you.

Phase Two: Practicing Your Skills

You are done with the first phase of Telekinesis. That is the time zone recognition phase. In this phase you have to practice simple skills that you have. As a beginner, go through this breakthrough of six steps that will actually initiate and help you in practicing your skills.

Step - 7:

To start, you should put your concentration to the objects which are small and not any other thing. Moving of the things that are around your vicinity is the basis of Telekinesis. For you to have a proper channeling of the energy in your body to this object that is near you, you ought to have a very hard concentration on it. The best objects to start with here can be a pencil or a match stick. You should also understand the fact that the more the molecules are apart in the system the easier you can make a manipulation to the system. Using these objects as a start is recommended where you can then progress to big things like chairs.

You should aim at practicing all these steps twice daily. This should sum up to about an hour of practice. Make a visualization of the object moving. It can be to your right and left. It can also be while being pushed pulled scooting or rolling. Visualize the entire object is being moved or only a single side is moving. Aim at getting a specific answer.

Step - 8:

After successfully succeeding in the above step, you can progress to this step whereby it entails making psi balls. This is a ball made of energy that you can manipulate, feel, and as you progress while making it you can take it to tasks that are complicated. While you have your hands well held within your stomach, have a feeling of the energy at your center. Hold your hands such that they should appear like they are tightly holding a ball. You have to visualize how big the ball is, its color, whether it is radiating and once you have made one that is concrete move it around and then make it to grow in size and shape.

By so doing you can now use this ball to diverge energy to other things and objects. Such that in the similar way baseball knock over a container the psi ball that you have created can also punch into objects in the real life situation; giving effects that have the same impulse with real life balls.

Step - 9:

In this step you will progress to the use of the flame-work. Such that as an additional exercise from the use of the objects that arte small you will work with fire! Here you have to put on a candle and watch it while glowing. Then you should clear your mind though the steps explained in phase one of this guide and let only thoughts about the flame of this candle fill your mind. Watch it while it is flickering and moving. While having all your focus on it, let it move by the use of your own energy. You can move it left or right, pushing it downwards or stretching it upwards. You can also glow it dimmer or brighter, aim at making it all yours! Does the flame behave in the way you want it to behave?

Manipulating flames can actually be a bit very easy. This is due to the fact that flames are balls of energy that are already made which quite lesser weight when compared to objects which can initiate a fight. This is the best exercise to use during the situation when you are feeling tired to assist in picking you up.

Step - 10:

You can now progress to switch-up exercises. Due to the fact that you are dedicating much of your time on a daily basis to perform this exercise; which is nearly an hour, try to switch it up by trying as many exercises as possible, you will never know the ones that will or won't work until you put a trial on all of them. The following ideas can assist you for this case:

Have a trial of the bending technique for the classic spoon. Ensure that you are not using your grandmother's china one! By holding the spoon horizontally in front of you by your hands, ensure that the curve of the handle is pointing upwards. In your center have a focus of the psi ball, and let it to get brighter and brighter while becoming hotter and hotter. By your means, let the ball move into your arms and then to your fingers, here your fingers will bend the spoon just like butter. It is important to understand that you should do this when you feel the ball is very hot.

Try poking an object that rolls on a table and then concentrate on it while zooming from corner to corner of that table. Do this daily while reducing the poke and maintain the focus which then will push it.

Get a compass and ignore all the science of magnetism in it. This can be very easy way to try Telekinesis as the compass floats freely. You should then put a concentration on it while your eyes are open or closed. Have a waving of your hands on it through the direction you wish it should move. When you are closing your eyes ensure you have a camera that is monitoring it or another person to monitor its movements.

Step - 11:
After succeeding on the step above, you can then progress to put a trial on the astral projections. This is a technique where you initiate "out of body experiences" these are the OBEs. Here your soul moves away from your body. It then ventures to the astral-plane. This will require a vibration state or hypnosis of the deep state. You should then have a mind that is very serious unto business matters. By this you will be able to move your soul from the body and then to the world that is around your vicinity.

It is good to understand that this is a very hard step to undertake. To ensure that you are not ending up frustrating yourself, start by doing the small bits. By this, I mean that you can put a trial in moving your leg or arm then have an out of limb experience that is very short. From there you can then try to move your whole "self". Try to warder from rooms to rooms.

Then you should relax and let your soul return to your body, although it can be daunting.

When you feel you are tired either mentally or physically you should stop. It is highly advisable that you should never continue doing this until you feel your fatigue has returned back to normal. This is just like sitting an exam when you have had 10 Red Bulls, slept for only two hours and there is a person who is smacking his gums behind you in the exam room. You can never do well o such an exam. If you have a rest you will be assured of better results. Ensure that you listen to your mind and body.

Phase Three: Understanding The Science

This is the last phase in Telekinesis for beginners where you have to understand the science behind it. Such that you should be able to define what Telekinesis is, and the science involved. You will be able to recognize and feel the energy in your body and use it to manipulate things by directing it to them. The following steps will help you get through it in a very simple way.

Step - 12:

In this step you ought to understand how you can be helped by Telekinesis and the ways of making it possible. Bearing the fact that energy is defined as the capacity to do a certain work, and also the change responsible to a given body's motion or state. In our body there is continual running of energy throughout. This is the energy that is responsible in keeping us working, breathing or moving. Obtained in form of chemical energy from foods and foodstuffs that we eat it is calculated in calories. For the case of our muscle cells, about 40% of this chemical energy is the only energy used for mechanical works. All the other potential energy in chemical form that is released through respiration of the cellular undergoes conversion to form kinetic energy. Thus rather than using the kinetic energy that is physical and seen in moving such things, we can as well use the energy stored in our bodies in the chemical form. This energy is present despite the fact that it can never be seen by the use of our naked eyes.

Here we have to let the thermodynamics rule apply. To explain it further, this rule states the fact that energy can never be destroyed nor created although it can easily be converted from a given stated to another. This means that for any given system and all the things in its surrounding there is a constant energy present in them. Whether such a system absorbs energy from the surrounding or give away a portion of the energy present in it, it will always have a constant total energy.

As opposed to the beliefs that have been present for very many years, there is no any magic with Telekinesis. Basically this is the transfer of body energy to the surrounding and then to the object that is around us in form of a system.

Step - 13:
This step involves recognition and feeling the energy that is flowing throughout our bodies. The center of this ideology is to ensure that you feel there is a

connection between you and the object around you together with the surrounding. Initially we said that you should visualize a system whereby "your body and the object" are connected. Here you should recognize the fact behind it and have the feeling in you. Carr out the following two exercises to achieve this:

With inclusion of your fist for about 10 seconds have a flexing of each and every muscle in your arm. It can be either the right or left arm. When the period is through relax your muscles back and feel the heat that is moving in it. This heat is almost like an electric sensation or even a pulse. The feeling when you have been contracting your muscles is the energy. Here you are seeking to obtain that heat/energy without moving your muscles or initiating a trigger. When you are able to do this you can then easily have sustenance of energy controlled emissions which are not like bursts.

The second exercise involves getting to a place where there is cold or ideal conditioned area. Here you should then relax your body, ensure that you are in position to sit or lie without even your hair standing up. This exercise is meant the energy that is used to perform things that are useless, as you will be able to control yourself naturally from the heating up or freezing your body. The longer you practice the better. You can in turn send all this energy through a section of your body, which can be the arm or chest or even legs to any other part of the body when it demands.

Step - 14:

This step calls for being very clear on the way you want to manipulate your system. You should make a decision on whether to pull, spin, or push the system. For each of the given option there is an approach that you ought to follow, to change levitate or change the state of the given object as follows:

In the case of pulling it is quite easy as you have the idea as to the direction in which you want the energy to flow.

Levitating can be quite hard. Here you have to focus in reduction of the inertia of the given system. This will make it light enough to offer reaction of the system electromagnetism as well as its surrounding.

For you to change the state of a given system you first of all ought to change the total kinetic energy that is present in the system. This is normally referred to as heat. One calorie with is the amount of the heat energy is equal to 4.184 joules. This is the required heat that can be able to raise the temperature of a gram of water by one degree-Celsius. For the cases of other substances like glass or metals we have specific heat values that are relatively low. This is why it is quite hard for the mind to change a given state of an object.

Step -15:

This is the last step but very important. Here you should aim at focusing that energy and then directing it to the given system. It all depends on you for the way that you will choose to do this. Just like the way different people have got different thinking ideologies, this method performs very differently to different people. You should maintain your focus on feeling system and paying attention to the weight that is present in it. Then make a decision as to the amount of energy that will be required to move this object. After this rate the energy with that which is present in your body while you are not touching it.

It is important to remember the fact that there is continual flow of energy needed for you to keep changing the object. Maintain a focus of the energy on it to ensure that it is not returning to its initial state. Other objects to use include aluminum ball- made from crumpled foil, wooden floor, glass marble, feather, low voltage light bulb as well as potato chip bag.

Caution:

You should not focus on a single task for a very long time, to reduce chances of headaches.

Made in the USA
Coppell, TX
26 February 2025

46460780R00015